# Our Papa is Santa, Too?

BEN HARPE

Copyright © 2018 Ben Harpe

All rights reserved. No part(s) of this book may be reproduced, distributed or transmitted in any form, or by any means, or stored in a database or retrieval systems without prior expressed written permission of the author of this book.

ISBN: 978-1-5356-1517-4 (paperback)
ISBN: 978-1-5356-1514-3 (hardcover)

# Also by Ben Harpe

*Squirrel Tales to Game Trails and Shore Lunches:
A Sharing of My Hunting and Fishing Experiences*

# Introduction

Ben and his wife, Georgiann, are retired and currently live in Kentucky. They have two grown children; their daughter, son-in-law, and two "fabulous grandsons" live in Tennessee, and their son and daughter-in-law live in Scotland. Ben retired in 2008 after more than forty-two years in the aviation industry. One of the primary reasons for his decision was making time for his family, and now, with two grandsons, it was a great idea.

This is not Ben's first attempt sharing his personal feelings and experiences on subjects near and dear to him. He is the author of Squirrel Tales to Game Trails and Shore Lunches, a sharing of his hunting and fishing experiences. His writing contains a genuine, "down home" honesty and a generous helping of humor and is seasoned with just the right amount of emotion and sentiment. Young and old alike will find his stories interesting, enjoyable, and entertaining. Ben not only writes from personal experiences, but also from the heart, and by doing so is able to share his unique love and respect for all life.

Like Ben says, "I only have to convince the children. The adults should know better." But he never refuses a request for a picture with Santa from anyone, adults included. Merry Christmas.

# Preface

When our daughter asked me to be Santa Claus for our first grandson, our little grandson Jeffrey, who loves me, and I love him, how could I say no? I couldn't. I told her I would rent a Santa suit, wig, and beard and plan accordingly to be available for when she wanted me to make my "appearance" for Jeffrey. She said "No, Dad. You can rent a Santa suit, but I want you to let your hair and beard grow out, so it'll be the real thing." Surprise.

My hair has been white for quite a few years. Being an old Marine, I always kept my hair neatly cut and short. I had no idea what my beard would look like, although I suspected it would be mostly white, also. Throughout my entire career, and raising our two children, I had never had any facial hair. Even our son asked, "Is that you, Dad?" when we met him at the airport some months later.

Thus, began my most recent Santa Claus venture. And it has been more fun than I ever imagined it could be. So please sit back, relax, and enjoy, from my perspective, what it's like to be Santa Claus. I think you will be surprised and amazed at some of what I have seen and heard. I know I am. And that's exactly why I decided to write this book. You just can't make this stuff up.

# Acknowledgements

My sincere thanks to my father and mother, God rest their souls, my wife, Georgiann, our daughter, Kyle Marie, our grandsons, Jeffrey and Evan, and our son, B.J., for all the wonderful memories. It's easy to be Santa when you have awesome elves like Jeffrey and Evan believing in and loving you.

And here's a special "Thank You" to all the children, and adults, who believe in Santa Claus. I'm proud of you and truly enjoy talking with all of you when we meet. I look forward to seeing you again. Merry Christmas.

Santa

Dedicated to Kyle Marie, Jeffrey, and Evan.

I Love You.

Papa Santa

# Contents

1. Where Do I Start? ...................................................1
2. Santa Came to Our House Every Year .........................5
3. Christmas in Vietnam ...............................................9
4. Christmas While in College .....................................13
5. Santa Claus Came to Our House ..............................17
6. YMCA Indian Guides and Indian Princesses .............19
7. Watching Our Children Grow Up .............................21
8. Watching My Parents Pass Away .............................25
9. Raising Our Children Without My Parents ................29
10. Santa Came to Our House Every Year, Too ..............31
11. "You Have to Spend Christmas at Home" .................35
12. Will You Be Our Santa and Easter Bunny? ...............39
13. It's Not Always Easy to Be Santa ............................45
14. Dad, Will You Be Santa for Jeffrey? ........................49
15. Will You Be Santa Claus for Us? .............................53
16. If You Are Going to Be Santa… .............................57
17. "You Look Like Santa Claus" .................................61
18. "I Should Have Known That" .................................65

# Contents

19. "He's Wet" ..................................................................69
20. "Thank You, Santa…" ...............................................73
21. Santa in Plain Sight ..................................................77
22. Santa Is Santa Is Santa .............................................81
23. "I Knew It, I Knew It, I Knew It…" ........................83
24. "You Would Make a Good Santa" ...........................87
25. So What Do Jeffrey, Evan, and
    All My Fans Think? ..................................................89

# Our Papa is Santa, Too?

# 1    Where Do I Start?

It's probably best that I start by saying I am the oldest of eleven children that our mother and father raised. I only mention that to confirm that I was once a child myself, many years ago, and as such believe I am qualified to speak from that experience. It was certainly a different time, "back then," but it was a very caring, loving, and memorable time, too. It was a time that nurtured and molded all our lives in many ways. To this day, I find myself practicing the very basics of life, family life, and social manners my parents taught me at a very early age.

One of my siblings passed away as a baby so there were ten of us, plus Mom and Dad, that shared a very small four-room house, including the basement, until I left home after graduating from high school. To say the least, we were quite close, or, as others would say, crowded. We were. No doubt about it. It's probably a good thing that most of us were boys and could use the outhouse when everyone was trying to get ready to go to school in the morning. With eight boys and two girls, you know who had priority in the one-bathroom house. Since the outhouse was not heated, and it was quite drafty and cold during the winter months, none of us boys spent any more time in there than was necessary to complete our pressing business.

# 2                                                       Where Do I Start?

The only thing worse than the bathroom situation, not that overcrowding wasn't bad, was that we had no running hot water. None. None for baths, none for laundry, and none for washing dishes. None. All hot water was heated in pans on the stove and was used sparingly. With such a large family, Mom did laundry every day and heated the water on the stove. When it came to bath time, you guessed it; she heated the water on the stove. And even at that, it was never a "hot" bath, especially if you were the third child to use the same bath water.

Dad worked two full-time jobs, and that included the weekends, while Mom worked full time taking care of raising us, and that included the weekends, too. Between the two of them, they kept us fed and clothed and playing outside, if the weather permitted. There was no room for playing in the house.

All of us kids had specific chores we did, depending upon our age. We all had to "clean up after ourselves," including dirty laundry into the hamper, dirty dishes into the sink, putting your own clean laundry away, dusting, vacuuming, changing younger sibling diapers, baby-sitting the younger siblings, and, as we got older, helping earn money for our school clothes. And there was no such thing as an allowance. I did all of these, since I am the oldest. Being the oldest, when I was thirteen, my Dad recruited me to help him in the garage in the evenings and on the weekends. As such, I "grew up" with my Dad and we became very close. He taught me a lot about growing up, life, living, mechanics, honor, integrity, and responsibility. He only had a sixth-grade education, but he is still the smartest, hardest-working, and most devoted family head I have ever known. I miss him.

While Dad earned the income, Mom managed it to ensure all bills were paid and that we had enough to get by on. She ran the house, as meager as it was, to make sure we had clean clothes, enough to eat, bag lunches for school, clean

# Where Do I Start?

bedding, clean bodies, and clean spirits, by getting all of us to church on Sunday mornings. I miss her.

We learned good work ethics and habits by observing Mom and Dad every day. I do believe that I probably had it better than my siblings because I learned so much from my parents while I was growing up. My siblings also learned a lot from them, but I learned a lot about how to be a good husband, father, role model, and now grandfather. I learned that, as the oldest boy, I always got new or used clothes every year while I was growing up, and my younger brothers got my hand-me-downs, many with patches on them. As I grew up, I worked all summer to earn money for my school clothes for the same reason. It was a great lesson, a lesson too many times lost on today's youth.

During my teenage years, my Mom and Dad managed to save money to start building a larger home for our family. It would include running hot water and sleeping arrangements to accommodate all of us. Once again, my Dad recruited me to help build the new house. We, and a couple of his brothers and one of my cousins, provided most of the labor. It took us several years to build it, but it was well worth it. And it was very nice. I didn't say fancy, I said nice. And it was their "new home."

I left home a month after I graduated from high school to join the Marine Corps. That was in July 1967. They moved into their new home over Thanksgiving weekend in November 1967. I was very happy for them. By the next time I got home, they had torn down the only home I had ever known. My youngest sibling started kindergarten in September 1967. They were all happy to be in the new house. My siblings were especially happy, since it meant more room and food at the table for them with me gone.

I can't help but believe that my family and childhood had a little influence on my becoming a Santa Claus many years later. Our raising a family of our own certainly added to that influence years later. And then came grandchildren.

Ho Ho Ho Ho Ho.

# Our Papa is Santa, Too?

## 2 Santa Came to Our House Every Year

By any definition, our family was poor. All of us children didn't know it and would not have understood it if we did. We were poor, but Dad and Mom worked even harder to provide for us. We never went to bed hungry, we always had a warm and dry place to sleep, and we always had enough clothes to be presentable when we went to school and church. As soon as we got home from school each day, we changed into our "play clothes" so we didn't damage our "school clothes."

Mom and Dad always made a point of celebrating our birthdays, complete with a homemade birthday cake, sometimes with ice cream, and always with a chorus of "Happy Birthday to You" and blowing out the ceremonial candles. There was also usually a small gift of some sort, typically something practical and useful, like a new shirt or a pair of shoes.

The birthday boy or girl was usually asked if they had a special request for dinner on their birthday, and then Mom would try her best to make our favorite meal for our birthday dinner. This was all in an effort by Mom to help make us feel special on our special day. It worked.

# 6          Santa Came to Our House Every Year

In my case, I was born on the birthday of one of my uncles, so we usually celebrated our birthdays together. My Mom and Dad would make his favorite meal, which he often provided, and we would share the cake and ice cream. He passed away while I was in Vietnam. I miss him.

We also always celebrated all the traditional recognized holidays. Of course, the Easter bunny always left Easter candy for us, and we always went trick-or-treating in our neighborhood on Halloween, weather permitting. And Thanksgiving was always a cause for celebrating because we had so much to be thankful for.

But when it was Christmas time, we couldn't wait for Christmas day, opening presents and all the excitement and good food. We were never disappointed, either. We always had a beautiful tree with an angel on the top and colored lights. And although none of us ever saw Santa Claus, he always stopped at our house and left presents for everyone. Christmas morning was always special, and, with such a large family, a truly wonderful time when we could all be together. We all got a present or two, and they were usually something practical and useful, like a new winter scarf or a new pair of gloves. There was usually a large box of Christmas candy to be shared by all, and we all had our favorite pieces. It was fun.

Christmas took on a whole new meaning as we grew up, left home, and had families of our own. It became more special when we could spend Christmas together and the grandchildren could be there and all of us were able to "come home for Christmas." These were all cherished times and made for many wonderful memories. Santa always found us, and left Christmas presents for us, wherever we spent Christmas.

By any definition, we were poor. We were also blessed with each other. Mom and Dad did a great job of providing

# Santa Came to Our House Every Year

everything we needed and raised us to appreciate all we had and to be thankful for it. I miss them both.

Do you think Santa Claus coming to our house every year had anything to do with my becoming a Santa Claus many years later?

Ho Ho Ho Ho Ho.

# Our Papa is Santa, Too?

# 3   Christmas in Vietnam

After graduating from high school, I spent the next four years in the Marine Corps. I spent the first three years at duty stations in the USA, and then I got "orders." It was my turn to go to Vietnam. So, I did. I spent the next eleven months "in country," which included Christmas. Obviously, I would not be home for Christmas that year. Christmas in Vietnam was not at all like any previous Christmas I had experienced. It also wasn't like any previous Christmas my Mom, Dad, and siblings had experienced, with me not there.

It was 1970 and there were no computers, emails, cell phones, and communication technology like we have today. We usually communicated back and forth by written letters through the mail, and it could take a couple of weeks for mail to be delivered. I say usually because it was possible to actually "call home" using ham radio operators in the States. The phone conversation was awkward at best and limited to only a few minutes, if the connections worked at all. Over! I did call home one time while I was in Vietnam only to find out that my Mom was in the hospital and Dad was there visiting her. Timing, huh? Over!

I wrote letters home and Mom wrote letters to me. Many times, my younger brothers and sisters would include a note to me in with my Mom's letters. It was always good to hear from home, but since none of them wanted to make me worry, they didn't always tell me everything that was going on there. Of course, that worked both ways. I didn't tell them everything that was going on in "my world" either. They saw and heard enough about it on the evening news every day. And besides that, we were not allowed to mention a lot of things we were involved in anyway.

We could receive "care packages" from home, so Mom would send me one every month or so. They also came through the mail, were expensive to send, and took at least two or more weeks to arrive. It was common for my Mom to ask me in a letter if I had received the package she sent me. It would eventually arrive, I think? I always enjoyed her homemade cookies even if they were only crumbs by the time they arrived. She would often include small gifts and I really loved her motherly thoughts that went into these care packages from home. They were always carefully packed with a lot of motherly love. I miss her.

Did you notice that I didn't mention my Dad relative to any of these communications? He was there, and he anxiously awaited every letter I wrote home. Mom said he would read and reread every one of them. He just couldn't bring himself to write to me, even though we were very close and never had any trouble communicating with each other and could talk for hours about common interests.

We also had something else in common. My dad had served in the Army and fought in World War II. He was wounded at the Battle of the Bulge and never talked much about his wartime experiences. He did not try to stop me from enlisting in the Marines, but he worried a lot about me the entire time I was in the service, and especially when I was in Vietnam. He was very relieved and happy when I left Vietnam and got out of the Marine Corps.

My Christmas 1970 "care package" contained the usual goodies, notes, pictures, news clippings, and a special

# Christmas in Vietnam

present, complete with instructions. Cassette-tape recorders and players were becoming popular and available at reasonable prices. When my Dad saw them, he bought two identical tape recorder/players and told Mom to send one to me for Christmas. They used theirs to record a message to me and then I would record a message back to them. Pretty smart, huh? It was always good to hear their voices. I have a picture of my Dad listening to a message from me. The note on the back is in my Mom's handwriting and says he would listen to my messages repeatedly. I miss them both.

All these years later, I still have that cassette-tape recorder/player. Unfortunately, none of those cassette tapes can be found and are probably lost forever. Wouldn't it be great to play that first Christmas message back and hear Dad's, Mom's, and all my younger siblings' voices? It would be wonderful, especially since Mom, Dad, and several of my siblings have since passed away. I miss them all.

Even though I was not able to be home for Christmas 1970, they and I were in each other's thoughts and prayers. We were together for Christmas 1971 and it was an especially memorable gathering with a lot of celebrating and blessings. In fact, a friend of mine that I served with in Vietnam spent Christmas with us that year at my parents' house. A good time was had by all and Santa came to their house with gifts for everyone, including my/our friend.

Was Santa trying to tell me something?

Ho Ho Ho Ho Ho.

# Our Papa is Santa, Too?

# 4  Christmas While in College

I left home again to go to college about a year after I got out of the Marines. It was a good decision precipitated by a conversation I had one day with my Dad. We were talking while I was working on a truck and I mentioned how I hated working in a factory doing repetitive piecework. He said he knew how I felt. He had been doing it for over thirty years at the time. He also told me to do something about it.

He explained to me that I had a chance to do something that he didn't have. He said if I wanted to eat beans the rest of my life, do what he did and just keep doing what I was doing. He reminded me that I had graduated from high school, I had spent four years in the Marine Corps working on helicopters, and I had a chance to go to college and make a good living. He strongly suggested, and recommended, that I give serious consideration to going to college before I got much older. I was twenty-three at the time, and certainly before I met a woman, got married, and had any children. He was right.

Within the next few months I had managed to pass my college entrance exams, located a college that offered aviation-related courses, applied, and was accepted. That fall I was back in school and looking for part-time jobs, so I could stay in school and pay all my expenses. My goal was to get my mechanic's licenses in one year, go out and work for a few years, then come back to college and get an engineering degree. At the end of my first year, I had my mechanic's licenses.

It was a great plan and I was right on my schedule. Unfortunately, the airlines were laying off mechanics. When I mentioned this to Jim, one of my professors, he advised me to stay in school, get my engineering degree, and try again in three years. So, I did. And three years later I received my BS degree and was ready to go to work. That same professor, Jim, arranged an interview for me with a company in Dallas, and told me to get in touch with them to make all the arrangements for my interview, so I did.

Before I go any further, I want to mention that during those three years, while studying for my BS degree, working as many as five part-time jobs to pay for it, and sleeping once in a while, I also met a young woman, dated her, got engaged to her, and we were married about a year before I graduated. We've been married forty-three years and she is part of the reason I am writing this book. She is the mother of our two children.

The interview in Dallas went very well and they made me a good job offer. We accepted it and moved to Dallas, where we spent the next twenty-eight years and raised our two children. The advice my Dad and Jim gave me was spot on. I still eat beans because I like them, but now I put smoked sausage in them because I can. Thank you, Dad, and thank you, Jim. I miss both of you.

As for Christmas during those four years in college, I was able to go home for a few days the first year. The next three years found me spending Christmas Eve with my wife's family, and then my wife and I would drive all night to spend Christmas day with my family. It made for a couple very long nights driving, but it was always worth it. And Santa always came to both places each year. It's like he

# Christmas While in College

knew where we would be every year. It was always a great time with our families and created a lifetime of memories.

Ho Ho Ho Ho Ho.

# Our Papa is Santa, Too?

## 5 Santa Claus Came to Our House

My wife and I rented a house for the first year or so after moving to Texas. This was intentional and allowed us the time to decide where we would like to live in the area and let us get familiar with Texas, Dallas, and the lay of the land, so to speak. About eight months into that year, we went grocery shopping one morning and came home with a house.

Seriously. With groceries in the car and headed to where we were living at the time, we decided to stop and look at a couple display houses a local builder had opened in a new development only a few blocks from where we were living at the time. We ended up picking out a lot and a floor plan that would be our first home and our home for the next seventeen years. Both our children were born while we lived in that house.

Our first Christmas in that house was 1977. Our daughter joined us for her first Christmas in 1980, and our son made his appearance in 1982. The distance between us and our families, combined with all the ground-support equipment needed to travel with young children, led to us spending most of our Christmases as a family in our own home in

Texas. Vacation time was usually reserved for trips to see our parents for a week in the summer each year.

Santa always delivered Christmas presents to our good girl and good boy every year. One Christmas, when our children were only a few years old, Santa made a special delivery to them at our house, and he stayed long enough to get his picture taken with both of our children. And he even had a glass of milk and a couple of cookies with us. Then he left to deliver presents to more good boys and girls.

Santa was a cousin of mine and only six months younger than me. We grew up together and he and his wife were living and working in the Dallas area at the time. He was a Santa as a means of earning some extra income and had offered to make a stop at our house for our children. Of course, we agreed, and it turned out to be a lot of fun for all of us. My cousin has since passed away, and I miss him. I can only imagine what he'd have to say about me being Santa now. I suspect it would be Ho Ho Ho Ho Ho.

Maybe it runs in our family?

# Our Papa is Santa, Too?

## 6  YMCA Indian Guides and Indian Princesses

In today's world of political correctness, this program has, I believe, been re-identified, and in fact may not even exist anymore. In any case, our children and I were very active members for several years when they were very young. It was a terrific program and was intended to bring working fathers into closer involvement with their young children. It fostered togetherness between us and was obviously based upon a Native American Indian theme. It included various "tribes," scheduled meetings of tribe members within members' homes, a couple camp-outs each year, and various other activities where interaction between fathers and sons/daughters and other fathers and sons/daughters led to quality time together. It was a lot of fun and our children loved it, especially the meetings at our house and the camp-outs.

It was interesting to me, as a father of two young children, to be involved with these other fathers and their children. In some cases, the "hands on" activities were a challenge for some fathers. In other cases, it was clear that the father wasn't spending much time, if any, with his children. All of us had jobs, so we were at work all day. Most of us did our own yard work, so we were busy on the weekends, too. Some were not involved with their children in any outside activities, be it sports, dance, piano, etc. Some of us even missed important recitals and heard about it often and loudly. It was a real revelation for me to see how different all the fathers were while all our children were very much alike. And yet, I understood it, too.

My position as father even extended beyond our own daughter. One of her best friends from school didn't have a father figure in her life. He had passed away shortly after she was born. When our daughter offered to share me as her father too, so she could belong to our tribe and be in the program with us, how could I say no? I couldn't.

We were active in the YMCA Indian Guides and Indian Princesses programs until our children were too old to participate. It was a most enjoyable program, and like any such program, you get a lot more out of it if you put a lot more effort into it. I saw several children very sad when they were told they were too old to participate anymore. I saw several fathers looking for other programs to continue the involvement with their child. And, unfortunately, I saw several fathers glad the program was done so they could get back to work. In these cases, I couldn't help but feel sorry for the child and hoped they would get involved in sports or other team activities through their schools or churches. I especially felt sorry for the father because he was missing his child's growth and development, and, in some cases, the chance to be a positive influence in their lives.

So how does this affect me becoming a Santa? Easy. I love children and try never to miss an opportunity to make a child smile or laugh, or even encourage them to do the same with other children. Positive reinforcement was always showered upon me and my siblings as we were growing up. I consider it payback when I do it and hope I'm paying it forward to the children receiving it. Everyone likes to be told they did a good job, or thanks, or keep up the good work, even children. I especially like to throw in a big smile or even a hug. But then, that's just me.

Ho Ho Ho Ho Ho.

# Our Papa is Santa, Too?

## 7  Watching Our Children Grow Up

I consider myself blessed to have had a mother and father in my life and to have had as much time with them as I did. My youngest sibling is thirteen years younger than I am and therefore knew our parents thirteen years less than I did. That same analogy applies to our children and their grandparents on my side of the family. Our daughter was only five when my father passed away, and our son was only three. Our children barely remember him, let alone knew him. I know he dearly loved both. Our son was named after him, and me.

Nine years later, my mother passed away. Our children knew and loved her very much and she loved both even more. She had enough contact and interaction with our children over those years that both clearly do remember her and doing fun things with her. Even though it wasn't a long time, just think about how much they would have missed if they never knew her.

Now fast-forward to those children that don't have a father or mother, let alone grandparents, to teach them how to be children. I've heard it said that children do not come with operation manuals like new appliances, cars, or cell phones do. That's a fact. And isn't it scary? Now we wonder why children grow up with such problems and issues themselves, and then reproduce them. Who is teaching whom? Many children are missing the most important and informative years and life lessons that would serve them well the rest of their lives.

I started this chapter by saying, "I consider myself blessed...." I do. I knew my parents and they set many good examples for me and my siblings. I passed those examples on to our children, and our daughter and son-in-law, and Papa and Gi Gi, are now passing them on to Jeffrey and Evan. I consider all of them blessed, too.

My wife and I tried very hard to raise our children the best we could, while working hard to provide good educations for them. We believe our efforts were well worth our time and expense. They are both adults and married and our daughter and son-in-law have further blessed us with Jeffrey and Evan. The decisions on our part to provide the best we could for our children while they were growing up influenced our lifestyle, and, in some cases, caused questions of why some friends of theirs had something we didn't have. These questions led to good opportunities for us to explain to them why and our reasoning for doing so.

It doesn't matter to me if I am dressed up as Santa Claus or if I am wearing shorts, tennis shoes, and a golf shirt; if someone asks me for a picture with them, I always say yes. I love the children and totally enjoy seeing their smiles and excitement at being with me and getting their picture taken with me. If a smile, a hug, or a word or two of positive reinforcement from me makes their day, I guarantee it made mine. The same goes for the adults that want their picture taken with me. You would be surprised at how many adults, men, and women, will ask me for a picture with them. Is it the kid in them, do they really want to show the picture to their two-year-old daughter, or does it just bring back good

## Watching Our Children Grow Up

memories and make them feel good? Does it really matter? It doesn't matter to me.

I have watched our children grow up, I'm extremely proud of both, and I am their biggest fan. Now we have Jeffrey and Evan and they just love to see Papa and Gi Gi. I cannot begin to tell you how proud I am of both and how much I love both of them. I am also their biggest fan, right behind their mom and dad.

When our daughter asked me to be Santa Claus for Jeffrey, how could I say no? When a parent asks me for a picture with their child, how can I say no? When an adult gets so excited when they see me that they ask for a picture with them, how can I say no? When a group or organization asks me to be their Santa Claus for a function they are having, I check my calendar to make sure I am available, and if so, how can I say no? It just doesn't get any better.

Ho Ho Ho Ho Ho.

# Our Papa is Santa, Too?

# 8 Watching My Parents Pass Away

It is always difficult to watch a loved one pass away, and especially so when it is a parent you had very close ties with and they pass away at an early age. That was the case with both of my parents. I'm thankful for the times I had with them and disappointed that they didn't have more time to see their children grow up and to even see their grandchildren grow up.

I mentioned early on in this book that Christmas at our house was a very special occasion due to the size of our family and because it meant so much to Mom and Dad that we all be together, as many times as possible, as a whole family. They knew that we would start leaving home at some point, and that after that, it would be very hard to get everyone together again, if ever. They were right, but we children just weren't concerned with such matters at the time.

Our father had fought a couple battles with cancer in his life, but at age sixty-three, it took his life and took him from us. I miss him.

Our mother had a stroke at age sixty-two and suffered permanent physical effects from it. She suffered another stroke two years later and passed away from it. I miss her, too.

In both cases, my parents were always happy to talk to us, to see us, and to spend time with all of us, even while they were in poor physical condition. It was always difficult to explain to our children what was happening to their grandpa and grandma. My wife and I did our best to explain it every time it came up.

When my mother had her first stroke, she lost her ability to speak and to use her right hand. She had always had beautiful handwriting and was very frustrated because she could not speak or write.

The stroke did not affect her mind, and she was aware of everything around her, up until she had the second stroke and passed away. I mention this because she knew all of us, and our children, was always very excited to see us, and loved to be involved with whatever we were doing. Even when she played cards with us, she would cheat and laugh when we caught her doing it. And even though she couldn't say it, it was obvious in her facial expressions and hugs that she loved us all dearly.

After my mother's first stroke, we all made a point of going home to be with her for Christmas. Most of us were able to be there. When we arrived, one of my sisters took us all aside to "bring us all up to date on her condition." One of the points my sister mentioned was not to say anything about how the wrapping on our presents looked. Our mother, in true form, had insisted on getting every one of us a small gift, and she insisted on wrapping them herself, so that no one would know what anyone else was getting. Now remember, she had lost the use of her right hand with the stroke.

Christmas morning was as exciting as it had ever been. After we were all up and together around the Christmas tree, my sister started handing out the presents. She would hold one up and Mom would point to the person it went to.

# Watching My Parents Pass Away

It was obvious that Mom had worked very hard to wrap each present, and although it wasn't nearly up to her normal perfect wrapping job, it was great to see how well she had done and how proud she was of herself for even doing it. Great job, Mom. I miss you.

So once again, Santa had come to our house, and most of us were able to be there and be a part of that very special Christmas. I still have that present and I'll always remember how Mom helped Santa wrap it, just for me.

As Santa Claus, I hope that some of the children I've had my picture taken with can look back and remember a happy time in their life when Santa visited them.

Ho Ho Ho Ho Ho.

# Our Papa is Santa, Too?

## 9 Raising Our Children Without My Parents

I only mention this subject because I believe that, whenever possible, it is important that children know their grandparents and that the grandparents can know their grandchildren.

I did not know my Dad's parents. Neither did my Mom. My Dad's parents had already passed away before my Dad ever met my Mom. But, having heard a little about my Dad's parents over the years, I do wish I could have known them.

I did know my Mom's parents, but not well and only briefly. My earliest memory of both was when Mom and Dad would take us kids to see them at their house. They were already elderly, and both were quite frail at that time. They both passed away many years ago.

Knowing my parents as well as I do, I can't help but believe our children would have liked them, too. Knowing my siblings as well as I do, every time we get together and start reminiscing, stories get told and we have a lot of good laughs. Then, if our children are present, the question always comes up: "Did you really do that when you were kids?" And the answer is always, "Yes, and don't you ever think of doing it."

Over the years, our kids have heard a lot of stories about when we were kids growing up. Wouldn't it be great if they could have heard those stories with my Mom and Dad sitting there and able to validate them? In some cases, maybe not, huh?

If I, as Santa, had the ability to make that happen, what a great Christmas present that would be.

Ho Ho Ho Ho Ho.

# Our Papa is Santa, Too?

## 10  Santa Came to Our House Every Year, Too

And every year it was bigger and better than ever. We spent seventeen years in our first house in Texas, and then we spent eleven years in the next one, also in Texas. In that time, both our children grew up, graduated from high school, and went off to college. Where did the years go?

My wife collects Santa Clauses and has many fine examples from little to big, new to old, fragile to brick, simple to ornate and from many other countries. She has some that stay on display all year long. No, I'm not talking about me. But when it comes to decorating for Christmas, besides many Santa's, she has lots of lights, ornaments, lights, garland, lights, wreaths, lights, a Christmas tree, and lots of lights. And that's just inside the house. She also likes lots of lights outside the house. When we turn on all the lights at our house at Christmas time, the neighbors' lights dim, and the electric power company puts an additional generator on line to support our Christmas lights. And our electric bill proves it.

One year, at our second home in Texas, while our children were still in high school, the neighborhood decided that all of us would decorate our yards and houses entirely in the small white lights. So much for all those colorful outdoor net lights and strings of colored lights for the Christmas tree we had already invested in. I must admit that the finished product was very beautiful. My wife was especially proud of the fact that our indoor, twelve-foot-tall, artificial Christmas tree was decorated with 4,500 small white lights. There was, according to her, a light on every single little branch. After seeing it, I had to believe her.

My wife also exudes the same enthusiasm and excitement when it comes to shopping for Christmas presents for everyone. I only need to ensure she gets several items of her liking from me. I'm not complaining, mind you. In fact, I'm glad she does handle the rest of the shopping. She is always "on the lookout" for Christmas presents all year long. She'll say, "Do you think so-and-so would like this for Christmas?" Or how about, "I found this for so-and-so for Christmas." Good. And now that we have our two grandsons to shop for, Katy, bar the door. I do readily admit that I am almost as bad as she is when it comes to "watching out" for gifts for the two of them, and it doesn't have to be just for Christmas. "I got this for Jeffrey and this for Evan. What do you think?" I think they will like anything their Papa and Gi Gi get them.

And then it's the week before Christmas and my wife goes on her marathon gift-wrapping spree in the basement. At the same time, she is planning and preparing for the Christmas morning ritual feast. She says she is multi-tasking. I say she is not giving full attention to either effort. Case in point: she has been known to forget what she got for whom, and has, on occasion, even found that she forgot to give someone a gift she had purchased for them some year before. This dilemma usually works itself out eventually, one way or another.

And then the next thing you know, it's Christmas morning. I mentioned the Christmas morning ritual feast because that is the best way we have been able to describe it to anyone else. It has evolved, over time, to be exactly that; a ritual

## Santa Came to Our House Every Year, Too

feast. We don't even start opening presents until all the food is out, everyone is up and has a plate full of food in front of them, and my wife starts handing out presents. Of course, there will be pictures to prove who got what later. The actual act of opening gifts is never an out-of-control frenzy at our house. As we graze through the Christmas buffet, sampling all the goodies and loading up on our favorites, we stop periodically to open another gift and see what everyone else got. Eventually, the last present is opened and we all sit around and thank each other for our gifts and blessings since last Christmas.

Then we do some more grazing as my wife and daughter start cooking all the items they planned for our Christmas day dinner. By the time dinner is ready, most of us are not hungry anymore. Too much grazing and too much lounging around have kept any hunger pangs away. By the time dinner is over, we are already commenting on how fast Christmas has come and gone for another year.

Then the cleanup begins. It's almost as if we are trying to erase all evidence that Santa has made another stop at our house like he always does. It is time to return to normal and to start looking forward to the coming New Year. Oh, how the times change as we grow up, and yet we try so hard to honor old customs while starting new ones of our own. Sometimes we need to really work at keeping the true spirit of Christmas alive in our homes and families. It shouldn't be work. It should be fun and last more than a few hurried days each year.

Ho Ho Ho Ho Ho.

# Our Papa is Santa, Too?

## 11 "You Have to Spend Christmas at Home"

Or so goes the directive my wife gave our children as they were growing up. She made it perfectly clear to them that she didn't care where they were the rest of the year; they had to be at our house for Christmas every year. Oh, if it were only that easy to do, huh? And while it did work that way for a few years, I think we all knew that there would come a time when one or both of our children would not be able to participate in our family Christmas at our house.

Our daughter, son-in-law, and two grandsons celebrate Christmas at their home and my wife and I are always invited to spend Christmas with them. The grandsons bring back a lot of memories from Christmases past when our children were their age. The Christmas morning buffet and all-morning grazing are alive and well at their home, too.

Our son and daughter-in-law live in Scotland, so getting home to spend Christmas with us is very expensive and usually difficult to coordinate. When they can arrange their schedules, so they can come visit us, it is usually not at Christmas time. So, they celebrate Christmas at their home and we Skype or FaceTime with them on Christmas day, allowing for the five-hour time change, of course. Technology lets us be together to that degree and we are always excited about that. It sure beats a cassette tape and a few pictures "wishing you were here."

From Christmases past to our Christmases present, about all we can really do is try to keep those family traditions alive for as many years as possible. It will always be great if we can all be together for a few days at Christmas, but as families grow up, move away, and have families of their own, it becomes increasingly difficult to get everyone together in one location. Maybe that's why Santa makes "house calls," huh?

"You Have to Spend Christmas at Home." If only it were that easy to do, it would be great. I'm sure you can all think of many reasons someone may not be able to spend Christmas at home with their loved ones. I know I can. Remember my Christmas in Vietnam? What about all those, young and old alike, that are receiving medical care or treatment and are confined to hospitals and are unable to be home for Christmas? Think about their families and how they wish their loved ones were not in harm's way or not in hospitals and could be together at home.

During the 1980s and 1990s, I worked for an airline in Dallas, Texas. Our primary charity was the Ronald McDonald House Charities. In every city we flew to that had a Ronald McDonald House, that house was a recipient of not only money, but a lot of personal attention from our employees, too. Our employees tried to spend at least one day a month at the Ronald McDonald House at their location to provide, and even cook, a meal for all the family members in attendance at that house at that time.

If you are not familiar with the Ronald McDonald House Charities, please go online and Google Ronald McDonald House for much more information on what they do and how you may be able to get involved with them. Be prepared.

## "You Have to Spend Christmas at Home"

They are there to help children, and their families, as they go through serious and major health issues affecting children.

It was always difficult for me to participate in these events, but I did it because I had a family that was blessed and not going through the troubling times these families were going through. It didn't matter if we were cooking hamburgers on a grill or cooking a full-blown Thanksgiving or Christmas dinner for these families. It was the idea that these families were able to participate in a home-cooked meal without having to plan it, purchase it, or even prepare it. They were able to spend more time with their child and still enjoy a good meal during the week and during the holidays, even when they were far from home and unable to share in a family holiday tradition.

I was not a Santa at any of those activities, and I didn't hand out any presents, but I did come away from every one of them thanking God for all he had blessed me and my family with. I also came away from everyone with heartaches for children that had a lot of treatment to go through in order to get well, for children that would be permanently scarred for the rest of their lives, and for children that would never go home again because they were terminally ill. I have never felt so helpless...

For the beautiful young girl that never gave up in her fight against the cancer that ultimately won the fight.

For the beautiful young girl that would survive but would be permanently scarred from being scalded by boiling water while trying to help her mother hard-boil eggs to be decorated for Easter.

For the handsome sixteen-year-old young man battling an inoperable brain tumor who told me he hoped he would be able to drive someday. I hoped so, too.

# 38     "You Have to Spend Christmas at Home"

Even though there is only so much one can do regarding such situations, you always come away wondering what else you can do, if anything else. I know that every one of the children that touched my life, then and now, want to spend Christmas at home. God bless them all.

# Our Papa is Santa, Too?

## 12  Will You Be Our Santa and Easter Bunny?

Thirteen years ago, I was working for a company, doing my job, and minding my own business, when a woman from our HR department asked me if I would be the company Santa Claus and the Easter bunny. Up until that time, I had never been a Santa Claus. I had been an Easter bunny for

# 40      Will You Be Our Santa and Easter Bunny?

a prior employer, but that's another story. All I can think of is she must have seen that entry on my employment application and figured she had a "live one" with me.

After I gave her a very strange look, she explained that our company had two primary charities that we supported, one in Cincinnati, Ohio, and the other in northern Kentucky. The one in Cincinnati was an orphanage and the one in Kentucky was a Catholic Children's Home. She went on to say that Santa would also be expected to make an appearance at the company Christmas parties and that the Easter bunny would participate in the orphanage Easter egg hunt and party.

She than informed me that the company already owned a Santa suit, complete with a fake beard and wig, and that she was sure it would fit me perfectly. (It did, with a lot of additional padding.) As for the Easter bunny outfit, I would need to rent one each year. And then she began to beg me to do it and even pouted a little bit. I agreed to do it for all the children we were trying to help.

One of my fellow employees was able to help me a few times by being Santa when I wasn't available. He refused to be the Easter bunny though, so I was "it." He wasn't even fazed when I mentioned he would find coal in his Christmas stocking if he didn't help me, and he seemed to care even less when I told him the Easter bunny wasn't going to come to his house or leave any Easter candy for him.

Let me start by saying that being the Easter bunny is not at all like being Santa Claus. It's not even close to being the same. In the first place, the orphanage always coordinated, with our company, the date and time for the Easter bunny to be at the orphanage for their Easter egg hunt and party. Our company provided the "party," which consisted of pizza, soft drinks, fresh fruit, and all the candy needed for the Easter egg hunt.

## Will You Be Our Santa and Easter Bunny?

A few fellow employees would accompany the Easter bunny to help me get dressed in my costume, go up and down stairs, go through doorways, and pose for pictures, and in general keep me from falling over something and breaking my neck, or anything else. This Easter bunny never had any speaking parts, so that was a good thing. This Easter bunny also had trouble navigating the uneven terrain on the grounds where the Easter egg hunt was held, because it was almost impossible to see out of the over-sized head. It was also always very hot in the Easter bunny suit. But the children always loved it and that was why we did it. God bless them all and all the staff at the orphanage.

The company Christmas party was always a gala event held in a hotel reception hall venue. There was a social (happy) hour, a nice sit-down formal dinner, an appearance by Santa, and then music and dancing. Since alcohol was involved, there were no children present. My wife and I would slip away right after dinner for a quick change into the Santa suit and then I would wait for my cue to make my entrance. I would then help draw names for various gifts and help hand out awards. It was always a good time for all of us in attendance.

As soon as it was time to dance and socialize again, I would be requested to have my picture taken with lots of my fellow attendees. I never refused a request and continued to do it until all were completed. Then my wife and I would once again slip away for a quick change back out of the Santa suit.

However, it was always impossible to slip away, unnoticed, dressed as Santa Claus, through a hotel lobby and restaurant area to the elevators. At one such Christmas party, someone had announced that "Santa was in the building," and as we made our way to the elevators, children and adults from the restaurant came out to meet Santa and have their picture taken with him. We ended up pulling a large chair into the lobby and getting our pictures taken with any and everyone who wanted to. I won't ever refuse a child's request to talk to me and have their picture taken with me. Quite often I do have to remind their parents to take a picture.

The Christmas party at the orphanage was very much like their Easter party. We, our company, provided pizza, soft drinks, fresh fruit, Christmas cookies, a small gift bag for each child, and, of course, Santa Claus. Santa was there until the party was over, which was after all the children had been brought in, eaten their lunch, and then returned to their class rooms. This usually took a couple of hours because the youngest children came in first. When it was time for them to return to class, they usually posed for a group picture with Santa and then left the lunchroom. Within a few minutes, another, older group of children were brought in and we went through the same process over again. And when they were finished, a third, even older group of children came in and went through the same process.

Then the orphanage staff would want pictures of Santa and my helpers with them for later use in one of their newsletters. It was always fun to work with them and to be with so many children that needed a little happiness in their young lives. I hope I was able to help them with that.

The Children's Home was a little bit different. We still hosted the Christmas party, but it was always one evening and the food we provided was their dinner that night. They still had pizza, soft drinks, fresh fruit, Christmas cookies, and a small gift bag for each child, and, of course, Santa Claus.

The difference was that there were only about forty children involved and they each had a wrapped present specifically for them, by name. After they had all eaten dinner, Santa would call each child up, by name, one at a

## Will You Be Our Santa and Easter Bunny?

time, to personally hand that child his or her present. They would then return to their seat and open their present.

No photos could be taken. None. All these children had been removed from unsafe living environments and their parents did not know where they were. It was for the child's safety. I'm sure none of the children were aware of this, but it was necessary according to the law. I hope we were able to bring a little happiness into their young lives, too.

# Our Papa is Santa, Too?

## 13   It's Not Always Easy to Be Santa

Believe me, it isn't. I didn't include a Ho Ho Ho Ho Ho at the end of the previous two chapters for obvious reasons. You won't find any at the end of this chapter, either. When I visited those children, it was very hard for this Santa. It broke my heart to see all those young children with unknown futures, under those conditions. None of them had any say in being born, the conditions or family environment they were born into, or even their day-to-day existence. What say do they have in their future? Those children all started their lives with one strike against them. Here are a few more examples.

There was a cute little blond-headed girl, about three years old at the time, that hung on to Santa's leg the entire time she was in the orphanage lunchroom. She cried her eyes out when she had to leave the lunchroom. I have often wondered where she is today, how she has grown up, and if she has found a good home and is happy. She would be in her early teenage years today.

There was another young girl at the Children's Home, about five or six years old at that time, that I was very impressed with. While we were calling the names of children to come forward and get their present from Santa, she stood patiently a few feet in front of Santa and watched as other children got their presents and returned to their seats. She smiled and was clearly excited each time a name was called. I kept hoping we would call her name next. It didn't happen. When we got down to only a couple presents left to hand out, I thought to myself, "Oh God, I pray we have a present for her." Thank God we did. It was the very last present and I was so relieved when she came forward to receive it. She just beamed. She also said, "Thank you, Santa." She hadn't even opened it yet, but she was thankful for it.

She would also be a teenager today. I wonder where she is, how she has grown up, and if she has found a good home and is happy, too.

There was also a young black teenage boy at the orphanage that was very angry and was under close supervision by two adults always. He asked Santa for a 9mm pistol and a 12-gauge shotgun for Christmas. When I told him that wasn't going to happen, he said he knew I wasn't really Santa, anyway. When I reported his request to his supervisor, I was told that this young man had a long history of petty offences and a violent past and was only one more crime away from being put into juvenile detention, or even prison, depending upon his age and the crime.

I wonder where he is today, too. But in his case, I really wonder if he is even alive still. I just hope he didn't hurt anyone else along the way.

I took a break from being Santa after the company I was working for went out of business. As much as I enjoyed being Santa for the children, it was also getting a lot harder for me to do it. Maybe the children got the biggest break of all and are now in good homes, happy and growing up in loving families. We can only hope and pray they are.

Very recently my wife and I were at a restaurant with some friends of ours. There were a lot of people there at

## It's Not Always Easy to be Santa

the time, including several families with young children. None of the children gave me a second look, as far as Santa goes. Christmas was still about a month and a half away, so they were not yet being exposed to the decorations, music, presents, and all the advertising. The adults, on the other hand, were reminded that Christmas was coming soon as soon as they saw me. Mind you, I was not dressed as Santa, nor was I even wearing a red shirt.

One of the families consisted of an older man, a younger man, his very pregnant wife, and their young son that I estimated to be two years old. As they finished their dinner and were in the process of leaving, they started trying to convince the little boy that I was Santa. As they approached us, I spoke to the little boy and reached down to shake his hand. He stopped, but it was obvious that he didn't know who Santa was. He wasn't frightened; he just didn't know what was going on.

As the two men encouraged the little boy to sit on my lap so they could get his picture with me, my wife, quite innocently, spoke to the woman and asked when she was due to have her baby. At that instant, the woman burst into tears and quickly left the restaurant. Of course, both men followed her out with the child.

Everyone with us wondered what had just happened, and especially my wife, who wondered what she could have said wrong. While we sat there, stunned at the woman's reaction, apparently the men were able to console the woman enough to at least get her calmed down. Then the older man, I think her father, came back in, and apologized for what had just happened.

He explained that the woman was twenty weeks into her pregnancy and had, just the day before, been told by her doctor that there was no sign of life with the fetus and that they would take the baby two days later. She was scheduled for the procedure the next day. Not only had she looked forward to having another child, and carried it for twenty weeks already, but she now had to experience the grief of its loss of life, and had to carry it two more days, knowing it was dead. It was a terrible shock and loss for all of them.

He then left to be with her and the rest of the family. We all sat there in total disbelief, not able to even imagine what she and her family were going through. All we could do was say a prayer for her and her family. Obviously, the coming Christmas that had been filled with so many great expectations was not going to be the same for any of them, or us.

Our Papa is Santa, Too?

# 14    Dad, Will You Be Santa for Jeffrey?

# Dad, Will You Be Santa for Jeffrey?

I never gave another thought to be a Santa again until two years ago when our daughter asked me if I would be Santa for Jeffrey, her son and our first grandson. He was only one at the time and had slept through his first Christmas when he was only a month and a half old. Our daughter and son-in-law had taken Jeffrey to get his picture with Santa at a local store. According to our daughter, he didn't want anything to do with Santa and was quite opposed to all efforts to the contrary.

I must admit that Jeffrey and I have had a very close and special connection from the day he was born. He was only a day old when we first met each other, and I was able to hold him for the first time. From that day on, as he has grown up, he totally enjoys my company and I dearly cherish his. He loves his Papa and I love him. To put this in perspective, at his first birthday party, our daughter told me that I had to share Jeffrey. Jeffrey didn't want to be with anyone else. I encouraged him to go play with the other children and to even sit with the adults that wanted to hold him. He did, but not for very long and then he was back with his Papa.

I think that it has everything to do with our relationship as Papa and grandson, that we are so comfortable around each other, that our daughter asked me to be Santa for Jeffrey. It just happens to be a coincidence that I have white hair and experience as a Santa with children.

Of course, I agreed to be Jeffrey's Santa for the following Christmas. I told our daughter just to let me know what she had planned, and when, so I could rent a suit, beard, and wig and reserve it for as long as necessary. That's when she said I could rent a Santa suit, but she wanted me to let my white hair and beard grow out, so I would be more convincing. I reminded her that I had not had long hair or any facial hair since I was in college. My hair was already white and had been for a long time. I wasn't sure what the beard would look like.

# Dad, Will You Be Santa for Jeffrey?

When I started pricing Santa suit rental costs and availability, I quickly decided I could buy one for less money than the quoted rental prices, and I'd have it if I needed to use it again—maybe the next year? So, I did. I was well on my way to being Santa again.

As the weeks and months passed by, my hair and beard grew out quite nicely. Jeffrey seemed to take it all in stride and wasn't too concerned with it. I can only think that it was because he knew it was me and we saw each other often enough that he always recognized me as Papa. Plus, he is one very smart little boy. He has even questioned why he can't have a beard like Papa. He wasn't even two years old at the time.

As for the adults that know me…I got a lot of comments about how they didn't recognize me, how they liked the long hair and beard, how I looked good, and how I should be a Santa because I looked like one. When I explained to them that I was letting my hair and beard grow out, so I could be a Santa for our grandson, they all agreed that I would be a good one. Most of them didn't know that I had prior experience.

Ho Ho Ho Ho Ho.

Our Papa is Santa, Too?

# 15    Will You Be Santa Claus for Us?

With my decision to be an "authentic" Santa Claus came a lot of outside interest from friends, family, businesses, and total strangers. Whenever I was asked if I was available to be Santa Claus, I would respond by saying I was only doing it for our grandson. I really wasn't interested in doing any more than that. I already knew what to expect at big and/or private Christmas parties, and I didn't want to go there again. I still don't, but for several exceptions.

As I continued to get requests to be Santa, I would tell the people to give me specific dates, so I could check my calendar for availability. It was true, especially since my wife and I do a little traveling to visit our family and friends and don't want to lose sight of those commitments. In several cases, I did get dates from people, but we were already doing something else and were not able to be there on the dates they wanted. We never got to the point of talking about how much we would need to be paid. That is a good thing because I would have had to come up with a price for our appearance based upon what they wanted, how long we would be there, and any possible expenses.

Then one day my wife and I were having lunch with some very dear friends in Lexington, Kentucky, when a young lady with us asked me to be Santa Claus for them in Houston, Texas. I explained to her that I really couldn't and didn't think I could help them out. I knew her and her family and was very good friends with her grandfather. Her parents own a couple large businesses in Houston and celebrate Christmas in a big way every year. They have events for their families, employees, and customers and some are open to the public. I still wasn't interested in being a Santa for them.

Then she explained that they hire several Santa's each year and always have trouble finding good ones. She just knew I would be the best one. When I started to turn her down again, my wife got involved and asked what the dates would be. When our friend told us the dates, ten days straight, and

# Will You Be Santa Claus for Us? 55

that they would cover our hotel expenses and compensate us too, my wife said, "We'll do it."

Of course, my response was "What?" Then my wife explained it to me as follows:

"Let's see now, ten days in Houston in December versus ten days in Kentucky in December? And they are going to cover our hotel expenses and even pay us for doing it. This is an easy decision. We'll do it."

So, we did, and it was a very good time. It was a lot of work, too, but it really was a very good time. We did eleven events in nine days. My wife even participated as Mrs. Claus. Up until then, I was Santa and she was my support behind the scenes for getting me into and back out of my Santa suit.

In preparation for that commitment, I bought a second Santa suit and my wife bought her Mrs. Claus suit. Due to all the events, we had our costumes dry-cleaned every other day, just to have a fresh and clean outfit for our fans. And, since we were Santa and Mrs. Claus, there was a lot more interest in getting pictures with both of us than there was with the other Santa's. We were very popular with our fans and their families.

We also have some very good friends in St. Andrews, Scotland, that manage a hotel there. We were there in early November that year, and they wanted me to be Santa for their annual gala Christmas party. They were very serious about it and tried hard to get us to commit to being there. When I asked them for the date of their event, they replied, "Christmas Eve, of course." To which I replied, "That's Santa's busiest night of the year," and that I was going to visit millions of children that night, not the least of whom would be Jeffrey.

It was another easy decision. Since this all started out as a request to be Santa Claus for Jeffrey, how could we not spend Christmas with him at his house with his family? Santa had even built a special Christmas present for him and his new little brother. How could I not be there to watch him open it and play with it?

We were back in Scotland last year, and when we caught up with our friends at the hotel, I was asked again if I would be available for their annual Christmas party on Christmas Eve. After they heard about how successful we were as Santa and Mrs. Claus, and they saw some of the pictures, they were more serious than ever and asked us both to be there. I reminded them that Santa is always busy on Christmas Eve with prior commitments with all the children, and especially with Jeffrey and Evan. Who knows, maybe we'll be able to be there for Christmas someday.

Ho Ho Ho Ho Ho.

# Our Papa is Santa, Too?

## 16 If You Are Going to Be Santa…

You really need to like people and you especially need to love children. As Santa Claus, we have a reputation to uphold that has been built on hundreds of years of Christmases. Children only know Santa for a few years before they start to question his existence. Based upon my observations, at about three years old the children are starting to believe in Santa. By about seven or eight years old, they are beginning to question Santa's identity. As a child, they may have different ideas about us based upon what they have been told. Remember, they are learning from adults about everything in their world. You can always expect questions. You need to be quick on your feet with appropriate and convincing answers.

Years ago, when I was growing up, there was a man who had a television show. He would intentionally ask young children questions just to elicit their responses. Many of their answers were hilarious and would cause you to question where they might have heard that. It also reinforced the adage to watch what you say around children because they may repeat it. I've been there and done that with our own children, and I have the T-shirt to show for it. Although I don't ask children irrelevant questions, they will ask questions and they are seriously looking for an answer.

What may seem like a silly question to you certainly isn't silly to them. You can never tell what a child is going to say.

You need to be ready to be Santa at any time. I try not to wear red shirts, most of the time. Between my white hair and white beard, and my belly, I already look enough like Santa that I get a lot of second looks and comments from adults, all year long. A red shirt just highlights the image to children and adults.

Be prepared to be approached by more adults than children from February through October. Adults still see me as Santa in the off-season. The children, however, start to see me as Santa in November, December, and January. That's simply because the children live in a very small world where they are totally focused upon today and now, and maybe what they will be doing later that day, let alone Christmas many months away. They don't know what long-range planning is, yet.

I've had adults come to our table in a restaurant, while we are eating dinner, and ask if they can get a picture with me. I don't make a scene; I just say yes and do it. The next thing I know, there is another adult with the same request. Is alcohol involved? Probably. Just another good reason to let them have a picture and not cause an ugly scene.

I've had a woman stop at a yard sale where my wife and I were visiting with our neighbor. She arrived on the back of a motorcycle and asked for a picture with me.

I've had a man in a truck stop me in a parking lot to tell me his son has been bad and not to bring him any Christmas presents. His son was in the truck with him. His son was probably eighteen years old.

I've had waiters and servers in restaurants ask for a picture with me. And that happens in other countries, too.

The youngest child I had my picture taken with was ten days old.

# If You Are Going to Be Santa...

The "youngest" adult I had my picture taken with was a ninety-five-year-young woman. When I asked her when the last time was that she sat on Santa's lap, she said, "Ninety years ago." She made my day. I think I made her day, too.

I mentioned in an earlier chapter that I never turn down a request to have a picture with me. It doesn't matter to me if it's with a child or an adult. If you refuse, the person may be offended and may even get loud and cause a scene. It's not worth it. Let them take a picture.

My wife and I were in an elevator at a hotel one time with another couple. The gentleman was BIG, as in very large. He kept looking at me, but he never did say anything. When we got off the elevator my wife asked him if he wanted his picture taken with Santa Claus. He broke into the biggest smile and said yes, he would. The woman with him didn't want to be in the picture with us, but she did say that we had made his day. I hope so.

Adults are notorious for telling their children to "go say hi to Santa." That's OK with me. I always have time for children. In most cases, the parents will then join their child and I must tell them to take a picture of their child with me.

We were at a water splash park recently with Jeffrey and Evan and we were all enjoying a good time. A very tiny little girl walked up to me and quietly asked me if I was Santa Claus. I knelt and told her I was and then I told her she needed to go back to her family, so they wouldn't wonder where she was. She said OK and walked away. I watched her to see where she went and to see if it looked like they were with her. They were. An hour or so later a man walked up to me with her and told me that he had "put her up" to asking me if I was Santa Claus. I told him I knew there was an adult behind it because children her age really aren't interested in Santa. He told me that she was two years old. I asked him if he wanted a picture of her with me and he said yes.

Don't be surprised when someone, young or not so young, asks for a picture with you. Just do it and make their day. It could make your day, too.

And never pass up a chance to give a child a hug, if they want one. Both of you will feel a lot better. Come to think of it, that works with adults, too.

Ho Ho Ho Ho Ho.

# Our Papa is Santa, Too?

## 17     "You Look Like Santa Claus"

What do you think? Do I?

My wife and I were in Mexico a couple of years ago to attend a family member's wedding on January 30th. Even though Christmas had been five weeks earlier, it was still fresh in some children's minds. We were staying in a hotel on the beach, but to get to the beach, we had to walk past the hotel swimming pool.

The first morning we were there we were going to walk down to the ocean and "get our feet wet." As we passed through the hotel lobby, my wife told me she needed to stop at the front desk and for me to go on ahead and she would catch up with me. So, I did.

# "You Look Like Santa Claus"

As I approached the hotel swimming pool I heard a young boy say, "You look like Santa Claus." I asked him if he really thought I did and he said yes. By this time, two additional boys and a girl joined him. All were about the same age, give or take a year, and all were intently focused on me. So, what else could I do? I gave out with one of my hearty signature Ho Ho Ho Ho Hos and started to walk to the beach.

My Ho Ho Ho Ho Ho Ho got the attention of their mothers, who were sitting around the pool visiting with each other. Then the children started in with the questions: Why was I there? How long would I be there? Was Mrs. Claus there, too? What about my elves? Where were my reindeer and sleigh? With their mothers listening in, I chose to stop long enough to address their questions.

After I explained that we were there for a week of rest after an extremely busy Christmas, my wife walked up, and I introduced them to Mrs. Claus. Then the same little boy that started asking the questions asked me, "Who is in charge at the North Pole while you are in Mexico?"

By pure chance, I had a picture of Jeffrey with a great big smile on his face wearing a Santa-type hat in my wallet. I took the picture out and showed it to all of them, and I

## "You Look Like Santa Claus"

explained to them that Jeffrey was my head elf and that I always left him in charge whenever we were away from the North Pole. With that, they had no more questions for me.

Mrs. Claus helped each of them get a picture with Santa. Then she helped each of their mothers get a picture with Santa. By the time that was all done, Santa was wet from all the wet swimming suits. We finally headed to the ocean for some rest and relaxation, and for me to dry out.

These families were staying in the same hotel as we were, so we saw them at least once or twice a day. We even saw them in town a time or two while we were there. One of the mothers told me the subject of conversation at every meal was how Santa was staying in their hotel and what we had talked about that day.

On the morning of the day we were departing, my wife and I decided to have breakfast near the pool before we checked out. The little girl and her mother were already seated when we entered the breakfast area. When the little girl saw us, she picked up her food and came to our table to sit with us. Of course, her mother joined us, too. The little girl and I ate our breakfasts while she sat on my lap. Another picture or two and we said goodbye.

My wife and I checked out and all our bags were in a cab when we started to get in the cab, too. My wife was in the cab and I was almost all the way in when one of the mothers ran up to me and told me that her son, PJ, was having a bad morning and asked me to talk to him. PJ was the little boy who told me I looked like Santa our first morning there. What could I do? We needed to leave so we could catch a ferry. I did the only thing I could do. I got out of the cab and went and had a heart-to-heart talk with PJ. I reminded him that I always know if he's been good or bad, so he needed to be good, for goodness sake, or I wouldn't bring him any presents for Christmas.

His mother thanked me, I got in the cab, and we even caught the ferry. It all worked out just fine.

Ho Ho Ho Ho Ho.

# Our Papa is Santa, Too?

## 18   "I Should Have Known That"

Have you ever been somewhere and seen someone you know and wondered why they were there? I know it has happened to me and I also know it happens with children, too. And when it does happen, you just have to love it. This was one of those times and I'll never forget it.

Our son and daughter-in-law live in Scotland, so my wife and I go there to visit them a couple of weeks every year. They both work, so it can be difficult for the four of us to do things together, since they both usually have different days off. When all the stars do finally align, and they get the same day off while we are there, we try to make the most of it by doing something, or going somewhere, together. Such was the case during a recent past November.

The day was a typical first-week-in-November day in Scotland: clouds, a threat of rain, and just plain gloomy. I say typical because that seems to be the conditions about half the time in Scotland. These conditions, at that time of the year, tend to be a bit chilly for most people. When these conditions exist, we carry an umbrella and wear a lightweight jacket. You just go everywhere prepared for the worst weather.

On this occasion, our daughter-in-law suggested we go to an outdoor attraction in the area known as the Scottish Deer Centre. None of us, including her, had ever been there before. Based upon a small brochure I had picked up at a hotel, it sounded like it would be an interesting place to visit. The brochure also included their phone number and easy-to-follow directions to their facility.

Once we arrived there, we realized they offered a lot more to see than just deer. They had birds of prey and regularly scheduled performances by them. They also had otters, foxes, bears, lynx, wolves, moose, elk, caribou, reindeer, and lots of other types of deer. Lots and lots of deer.

The main building was where we paid for our admission tickets and could walk around looking at all the various indoor displays and related information. Part of our admission price included a map of the entire Centre so we could do our own self-guided tour of all the outdoor exhibits, know where we were, find our way back out again, and all, hopefully, without getting lost. I'm happy to report that it worked, too.

After we watched a birds-of-prey performance and then watched as the staff fed the otters, we were ready to start our self-guided tour around and through the facility. It consisted of large fenced-in areas, each of which had several species of deer in them. It also included a number of large enclosures, each of which contained a mammal of some sort, specifically, bears, wolves, lynx, fox, and other such critters. Each enclosure included a sign identifying its occupants and their regularly scheduled feeding time, so you could plan to be there at that time and see the animals awake, active, and eating, if you so desired. Believe me when I say the animals know when it's feeding time. They were anxiously awaiting the staff to arrive, on time. Access to all the areas was by well-marked and maintained walking paths.

## "I Should Have Known That"

The four of us had stayed pretty much together for our walking tour, most of the time. I had stopped at an enclosure that contained a beautiful red fox. He seemed to be as interested in me as I was in him. He sat still and listened intently while he watched me. I would talk to him and he acted like he was trying to understand what I was telling him. Maybe it was my white hair and beard that he was so focused on.

A tap tap tap on my right hip surprised me and caused me to refocus my attention on my surroundings. When I looked down to see what was happening, I saw three young boys, five to six years of age, standing there looking up at me. There were two women with them, but they didn't say anything. I assumed the women were the boys' mothers. Then one of the boys said, "What are you doing here, Santa?" Now, bear in mind that I was not dressed up like Santa.

My immediate response was to say hello to the boys and to tell them I was happy to see them. Then I looked at the women to make sure they didn't have a problem with their sons talking to me and me talking to them. I got no indication whatsoever, either way, from them, so I proceeded to answer the little boy's question.

I told them I had some of my reindeer there and that I was there to check on them and make sure they would be ready for Christmas. I asked them if they had seen my reindeer in their pens yet. I got that "deer in the headlights look" from all of them, no pun intended. I also told them that I sent my reindeer to the Deer Centre right after last Christmas, so they could get a lot of good rest after such a busy night of delivering gifts. I told them how they get very tired working so hard and that they need to have a place like the Deer Centre to rest and get lots of good food, so they will be ready for Christmas the next year.

Two of the boys had not said a word. The boy who had asked me what I was doing there, very matter-of-fact-like, slapped his forehead with the palm of his hand and said, "I should have known that."

I had all I could do to keep from laughing aloud. I looked at their mothers and asked them if they wanted a picture of me with the boys, just to keep from laughing. After a couple pictures, the boys and their mothers walked away. I think they were headed back to see the reindeer again. God bless them all.

Ho Ho Ho Ho Ho.


Note: If you are interested in more information regarding the Scottish Deer Centre, just Google it.

# Our Papa is Santa, Too?

## 19     "He's Wet"

Those are two words you never want to hear Mrs. Claus, or your elves say as they hand a child to you to sit on your lap for their picture with Santa. Now you know why Santa usually wears white gloves. Just remember that it isn't the child's fault and don't take it out on them. I have been known to inform the parent of a child's "situation," just in case they weren't aware of it.

Christmas parties with Santa are supposed to be a special time for the children, first and foremost. I agree. It's when the party includes pizza, cake, ice cream, and other messy foods that I usually find some children leave a "lasting impression" on their own Christmas outfits, as well as mine. Again, it's not their fault. I try to carefully maneuver them into poses that not only hide their "accidents" or stained outfits but also prevent getting them all over mine. Most of the times it works, but I have a spare suit for those times when it doesn't. I usually use a clean suit every day anyway. Thank goodness for "in by 9:00 a.m. and back by 5:00 p.m." same-day-service dry cleaners.

I have made many Santa visits by myself, but I prefer an assistant along, if for no other reason than just to help me get in and out of my Santa suit. Elves and/or Mrs. Claus also seem to help calm children down, just by being there to help the child or children get on and off my lap and to help pose them for a good picture. I can assure you that if the family and children have a choice of getting their picture taken with Santa or with Santa and Mrs. Claus, they will choose Santa and Mrs. Claus every time.

And finally, you can expect a few children will not want anything to do with Santa, let alone to sit on his lap long enough to get a picture with him. Believe me, it happens, and when it does, it usually isn't very pretty, let alone fun for anyone else.

After thousands of pictures with small children, I can only think of six times when I stopped the process to prevent further trauma to the child. In each case, the parents were determined their child was going to get his or her picture taken with me whether he or she liked it or not. I felt sorry for the child.

I had the parents take the child away from me and I explained to them that any picture of their child with me under those conditions would not be a picture they would be proud of and that it wouldn't look good as their Christmas card either. They agreed.

Then I suggested they step aside and let their child calm down while observing other children getting their picture taken with me. They could reassure their child that it was going to be OK to have their picture taken. Then, when they thought the child was ready to try it again, I would suggest that maybe they leave the child in their stroller, as an example, and just park it next to me for the picture. Or better yet, I would suggest that Mom or Dad hold the child and join me for the picture as a buffer between me and the child. Get creative and have a few options available. The child will be happy, the parents will appreciate it, and so will you.

## "He's Wet"

By the way…we were successful in getting good pictures with five of the six children and their families. The sixth family just took their child away and never came back to try again. I suspect the child was very tired and just wanted to go home. It happens.

Ho Ho Ho Ho Ho.

# Our Papa is Santa, Too?

## 20 "Thank You, Santa…"

My wife and I were in California in early January last year along with some friends of ours. We were there to see the Rose Bowl Parade and take a tour with a company we have used several times in recent years. It was a good time and we got to see a lot of California. Since I look like Santa Claus, the tour company asked if I would be willing to do a promotional photo shoot for them and provide an interview to accompany it. Like I said earlier, never say no to a request to have your picture taken.

Christmas was less than two weeks earlier, and a lot of places still had Christmas decorations up. The hotel where we were staying at the time was one such place. We did the interview and part of the photo shoot with a beautiful Christmas backdrop in the lobby of the hotel. The remainder of the photo shoot took place in the float-assembly barns prior to the parade.

While we were doing the photo shoot at the hotel, a family with three children asked if they could get a picture with me. Of course, I said yes. They thanked me several times after they got their pictures of Santa with them. I was not dressed like Santa, but it doesn't seem to matter, most of the time.

The photo shoot continued and when we were finished at the hotel, the tour group staff thanked us and left. They were complimentary of how we handled the request and I explained that it was just my job, in both their request and the family's request. That's what Santa does.

Before we left California to return home, my wife and I, along with our friends, were having dinner at a restaurant in San Francisco. It had been a good trip, but we were all ready to go home. The next morning would find all of us going our separate ways, so to speak.

As we were enjoying our dinners, the restaurant filled up with a lot of other customers. Since the restaurant required people coming in for dinner to wait to be seated, there were a few people waiting at the hostess station. We hurried to get finished with our dinner to free up our table so that one such family could be seated.

Before we were even done at our table, it became clear to us that this particular family had recognized Santa. The three children were especially focused on us and were paying particular attention to me. Please remember that Christmas had been less than two weeks earlier, so it was still very fresh in everyone's memory, especially the children's.

As we approached the hostess station to exit the restaurant, I went directly to the family as they watched in pure amazement. They were all excited about me even stopping to speak to them. The three children consisted of a young girl about five or six years old, a young boy about six or seven years old, and another young boy about seven or eight years old. Mom and Dad were speechless while the children just beamed. I asked their mother if she would like to take our picture together and she snapped back to reality. While she got her iPhone out and ready, I knelt with the children and we posed for a couple pictures.

As I knelt with the children, the lovely little girl said, "Thank you, Santa, for all the nice Christmas presents." Of

# "Thank You, Santa..."

course, I told her she was very welcome. Then I heard the two boys say thank you, also.

Then I stood up and told their mother and father that they were doing a great job with their children and how they were so polite and that they had thanked me for all their presents. I also told them to keep up the good work.

My wife and our friends, along with some other people, had witnessed this and were patiently waiting for me, so I said goodbye and we left. I hope I made their day because I know they made mine.

Several months later, we, along with these same friends, were on a Rhine River cruise together. The cruise was a tour with the same tour company we were with in California, the same tour company we had done the photo shoot for. While we were in the process of boarding the river cruise boat, the tour company awarded me with one of their bright-red company jackets with my name on it on the right side of the zipper and "Santa" on the left side of the zipper. There would be no hiding my identity on that tour. What a great "thank you."

Ho Ho Ho Ho Ho.

# Our Papa is Santa, Too?

## 21   Santa in Plain Sight

Having been a child myself at one time, I know that children don't usually get too concerned about anything much past today or tomorrow, let alone months away, such as Christmas. My two grandsons constantly validate my theory. Just ask Jeffrey what he had for lunch and he probably can't tell you. He's only three. Was he impressed? Probably not, unless it was a PB&J sandwich, which is his favorite. Is he even aware when it's lunchtime, at home or when his class stops for lunch? Of course not. His small world doesn't revolve around such things, yet. His world, just like most children's, revolves around the here and now, for the most part. They unknowingly rely on adults for almost every aspect of their short lives, including when and what they have for lunch. This will only change as they grow up and absorb many new things. Remember, everything is new to young children. Come to think of it, I don't remember what I had for lunch, either. Boy, talk about not being impressed, huh?

Think back to when you were a child, or even when your own children were young. Someone usually told you everything you needed to know for that particular day. It's time to get up. Wear this outfit today. It's time to eat breakfast. You can't play with that; you'll hurt yourself. Don't forget your books and your lunch. Go play outside. Have you got homework to do? There is no school tomorrow because it's the weekend. What's a weekend?

When people ask me if I ever get tired of the children thinking I'm Santa Claus, I explain to them that it usually isn't a problem. I tell them that if I don't wear a Santa suit, or wear a bright-red coat or shirt, I can walk through an elementary school and almost all the children will not give me a second look. Christmas is not on their radar until about mid-November, when the Christmas decorations are up, they start seeing Santa on TV, Christmas music is heard, and Santa starts making public appearances. From then until about the end of January or even mid-February, they will be more attentive to the excitement of Christmas and Santa Claus.

Once Christmas is over and all the Christmas excitement has subsided, they get back into their daily lives. This will last for about nine months, during which time they will be in school, out of school for summer vacation, on vacation, and back into school. They are not thinking about Christmas or Santa during that time. The teachers, on the other hand, are a different story.

Adults in general have no problem at all identifying me as Santa and can be depended upon to say something. That's just fine with me, and when asked if I am a Santa, I explain that I am, and then they have more questions or want their picture taken with me, no matter what I am doing or where I am.

I believe I only need to be convincing to the children and I can usually accomplish that. I don't worry about convincing the adults because they should know better.

Please note that I am careful to mention "usually." That is because there are always exceptions to everything. As an example, my wife and I were recently having dinner with my brother and sister-in-law in Kansas City, Missouri.

# Santa in Plain Sight

There was a young family already eating their dinner at the table next to where we were seated. I think it was Grandma, Mom, Dad, and their two small children. Both were little girls and I estimated them to be maybe two and four years old, at the oldest.

As we took our seats, the two little girls stared at me. Of course, I spoke to them both and they just continued to watch me. At one point I mentioned to their mother that when they were done eating and ready to leave I'd be happy to pose with them for a picture. She was thrilled and said they would. They were very well- behaved children.

We were almost done with our dinner when a lady walked up and was very excited about how those children were so interested in me. I carry small wallet-size pictures of Santa and Mrs. Claus for just such occasions, so I gave her one. She showed it to the two little girls and her excitement rubbed off on them. At that point, it was time for pictures with them.

Both little girls were positioned on my lap, one on each knee, and while their mother took our pictures, the oldest one told me what she wanted for Christmas. After they had their pictures taken, I gave each little girl a picture of their own of Santa and Mrs. Claus. They were very excited about that.

As they got ready to leave, I told the mother that it was very unusual for children that age to recognize me as Santa, especially since I was not dressed in my Santa suit. She told me that she and her husband read Christmas stories to their children all year long, and that Santa was a real favorite of theirs. Both the mother and father thanked me for making their daughters' day, and so much more with their own pictures of Santa and Mrs. Claus. How's that for an exception to the rule? Oh, and by the way, it was September.

Ho Ho Ho Ho Ho.

# Our Papa is Santa, Too?

## 22  Santa Is Santa Is Santa

Being a Santa Claus and traveling around the country, and the world, I am amazed at just how universal a figure Santa is. Even though many countries have different ideas of what Santa looks like when he is all dressed up for Christmas, and many have very specific customs relative to what Santa does during the Christmas season, Santa still generates attention wherever he goes, and, as discussed in the previous chapter, to some degree, year around.

During the "off-season," those nine months other than the Christmas season, I still get asked by adults if I am Santa, and I get the occasional "stare" from a child that thinks he or she may have just seen Santa. In the case of a child, I will usually wink at them and even speak to them to say "Hi, sweetie" to little girls or "Hi, buddy" to the little boys. I also try to keep moving, so as not to disturb any adults with them.

With adults, on the other hand, I acknowledge that I am a Santa Claus, specifically for the children, but not exclusively. That usually warrants a response something along the lines of "That's great" or "You make a good Santa" or "Can I get a picture with you for my two-year-old child at home?" and many more, including, "How much do you charge and do you ever do special events or parties?" I then ask them when and where their event is so that I can check our schedule to see if we are even available then.

The Rhine River cruise I mentioned in Chapter 20 took us through Germany, into France and Switzerland, and back to Germany. It was mid-April and very early May, so the Christmas season was over with. That didn't stop waiters, servers, other cruise passengers, and a few children from wanting a picture with Santa. My bright-red Santa jacket probably had something to do with it, too. It was no different there than it is here. Everyone who wanted a picture with Santa got one, including all the children and the adults acting like children.

Ho Ho Ho Ho Ho.

# Our Papa is Santa, Too?

## 23 "I Knew It, I Knew It, I Knew It..."

You just have to love it when you make someone's day, and I consider myself blessed in that I get a chance to do just that so often. I've already made it clear that I am an "old softy" when it comes to children and that I sometimes wish I could do more for some of them. But I must say, there are times when I make an adult's day and it leaves an impression on me, too.

Remember the ninety-five-year-young lady in Houston? I remember the couples in an elevator in Houston where it was the guys that wanted the picture with Santa more than the ladies with them did. And the waiters and servers in Cincinnati, Ohio, Germany, Switzerland, Scotland, France, Atlanta, Georgia, on the cruise ship, and in many more places. And then there are all the parents that point Santa out to their children, or even send them over to see me, in restaurants, public parks, and even just walking through a store or parking lot. I even have a "cult following" of adults, mostly women, at our church.

There is a very nice, sweet woman receptionist in one of the clinics at our local Veterans Administration Hospital that I get to see twice a year. I always look forward to seeing her because she gets so excited when she sees me. I have been known to stop by to say hello to her when I'm at the hospital for other reasons. When I gave her a picture of Santa and Mrs. Claus, she was very thankful and told me she couldn't wait to show it to her grandchildren.

Then there was an elderly gentleman walking with his young grandson early one morning along a breakwater in a small town in Scotland when I met them as I was walking in the opposite direction. I spoke to them as we passed, and they returned my morning pleasantry. Before we had gone more than twenty to thirty yards, the elderly gentleman called to me, so I returned to meet them about halfway. He apologized for interrupting my morning walk and excused himself for any delay while he thanked me for taking a few minutes to speak with him and his grandson.

I will never know why he decided he wanted to stop and talk with me, but it really doesn't matter, anyway. What mattered was that he wanted to get a picture of his grandson with Santa Claus. I was more than happy to accommodate his request and certainly hope he was, too. Perhaps we'll cross paths again someday.

My wife and I were coming through customs when we were re-entering the United States early last November. It had been one of the more miserable flights we have had in a long time. After eight hours on an airplane, and a long line in customs, it was finally our turn to speak with a customs agent. This agent was probably in his late twenties and was very formal about his duties. When we stepped up in front of him, he asked if I was ready for Christmas. "Of course," I said. Then my wife handed him a picture of Santa and Mrs. Claus. With that, he broke into a huge grin and started telling everyone in the area that he had a picture of Santa and Mrs. Claus, and that he couldn't wait to tell his children that he had cleared Santa and Mrs. Claus back into the country for Christmas. As we left, he was still telling everyone how he

## "I Knew It, I Knew It, I Knew It…"

had just talked with Santa. While we clearly made his day, I guarantee you that he made our day, too.

Another person I hope to cross paths with again someday is a young, as in half my age, black man that I crossed paths with in an elevator at our local Veterans Administration Hospital. I'm confident he is a veteran, like me, who has health issues related to his military service. Thus, who knows, we just might meet again. I hope so.

As it was, I entered an elevator to go down to the ground floor and this gentleman was already on the elevator. It was just the two of us and I had asked him how he was doing as I boarded the elevator. He looked at me rather strangely but didn't respond.

When the elevator stopped on the ground floor and the elevator doors began to open, he asked me if I was Santa Claus. I told him I was as I stepped out of the elevator. At that point, he started dancing around, still in the elevator, and repeating, "I knew it! I knew it! I knew it!" When the elevator doors closed, he was still in the elevator dancing and chanting, "I knew it! I knew it! I knew it!" I have no idea where he went from there, and I did not see him again after that. I obviously made his day, and I honestly have to say that he made mine, too.

Ho Ho Ho Ho Ho.

# Our Papa is Santa, Too?

## 24 "You Would Make a Good Santa"

I'm always flattered when someone tells me that I would make a good Santa Claus. It's one thing when it's a total stranger saying it, but it's really something else when it's someone who has known me for years saying it.

When a total stranger tells me, I would make a good Santa Claus, or that I look like Santa, I usually respond by telling them I am a Santa, and thanks for the compliment. Obviously, my long white hair and beard, along with the belly, is usually a good indicator that I may be a Santa Claus. Another good clue is when total strangers ask to have their picture taken with me or they send their children over to talk to me. In all these cases, it isn't Christmas time and I'm not dressed up in a Santa suit.

On the other hand, a couple of years ago, we attended a high school graduation party for a niece of ours. When we arrived, I had Jeffrey with me when we made our way through the garage, past the food line, and into the back yard, where a lot of people were eating, drinking, and visiting. A lot of people saw us, and it was clear to me that they had no idea who we were. I suspect some thought we were crashing the party. I took Jeffrey over to get him a drink and a cookie, to hold him over until we could get him introduced to everyone and then get him something to eat.

My sister-in-law didn't recognize us and didn't say a word until I spoke to her, at which time she recognized my voice and screamed out, "Oh my God. Dennis, it's Ben." That reaction startled Jeffrey and got everyone else's attention, too, including the rest of my family that was there. Then they noticed Jeffrey.

Then everyone there that knew me came over to visit, meet Jeffrey, and tell me how much I looked like Santa Claus. When I told them I am a Santa Claus, many of them were not surprised and said I make a good one.

When my best friend passed away a couple of years ago, my wife and I attended his memorial service in Dallas, Texas. He and I had worked together for eighteen years and had been friends for thirty-six years. I knew a lot of the people that we had worked with and who attended his memorial service. None of them recognized me. Not one, until I gave a eulogy for our friend. Afterward, every one of them made a point of telling me they would have never recognized me. Most of them wanted a group picture with me. It made me sad that our friend, my best friend, couldn't be in the picture too. Fortunately, my wife and I had spent several days with him and his wife just a few months earlier and we had taken pictures of us together at that time. He got a kick out of how I looked and so did his family. Even his youngest great-granddaughter, less than a year old at the time, was very agreeable to letting me hold her. She is a cutie.

Ho Ho Ho Ho Ho.

# Our Papa is Santa, Too?

## 25  So What Do Jeffrey, Evan, and All My Fans Think?

Based solely upon my observations and experiences, and my fans' reactions, I must conclude that I must be a convincing Santa Claus to the children and a lot of adults. That was my goal in being a Santa and I seem to have accomplished it.

# 90  So What Do Jeffrey, Evan, and All My Fans Think?

I know that Jeffrey and Evan love me for who I am: their Papa and a person who loves to spend time with them. They both show it by wanting to spend time with me, too. And I love every minute of it. Their reaction whenever they see us would indicate that they feel the same way about us as we do about them. It's because of our special relationship with each other that I decided to write this book.

I learned early on in my Santa Claus ventures that some of the most vulnerable members of our society are desperately looking for someone they can believe in and who will take the time to believe in them. And even though it's not always easy to be Santa, I certainly pray that as Santa, I was able to help them have a happy day among so many unhappy ones. May God bless them all, always.

As for the adults that I encounter and say that they should know better, could it be that they too had a childhood that was less than ideal? Could they be trying to fill in a missing page in their childhood years? Could it be that there was no Santa figure in their lives, and now that they are grown up, they want to at least get a picture of themselves with Santa? I don't know and I'm not going to worry about it.

Like I said earlier, never say no to a request for a picture with someone. And, never pass up an opportunity to hug a child and have a picture with them. They will be happy, and you will be, too.

So, in closing, I will continue to be Santa Claus to Jeffrey and Evan, and any other children or adults acting like children, for as long as they believe in Santa. I hope they will never stop believing in Santa Claus or their Papa. And in return, I'll never stop believing in them.

I love you, Jeffrey.

I love you, Evan.

I love all you children.

## So What Do Jeffrey, Evan, and All My Fans Think? 91

And may every day be like Christmas day for all of you.
Merry Christmas.
Ho Ho Ho Ho Ho.

www.ingramcontent.com/pod-product-compliance
Lightning Source LLC
Chambersburg PA
CBHW070155080526
44586CB00015B/1998